NEW YORK RANGERS

BY WILLIAM ARTHUR

Book design by Maggie Villaume
Cover design by Maggie Villaume

Photographs ©: Kathy Willens/AP Images, cover, 24–25; Ron Frehm/AP Images, 4–5, 7; Marty Lederhandler/AP Images, 8; AP Images, 10–11, 15; Bettman/Getty Images, 12; Ray Stubblebine/AP Images, 16–17; Ryan Remiorz/The Canadian Press/AP Images, 19; Bill Kostroun/AP Images, 20; Julie Jacobson/AP Images, 23; Elise Amendola/AP Images, 26; Adam Hunger/AP Images, 28

Press Box Books, an imprint of Press Room Editions.

ISBN
978-1-63494-494-6 (library bound)
978-1-63494-520-2 (paperback)
978-1-63494-571-4 (epub)
978-1-63494-546-2 (hosted ebook)

Library of Congress Control Number: 2022902273

Distributed by North Star Editions, Inc.
2297 Waters Drive
Mendota Heights, MN 55120
www.northstareditions.com

Printed in the United States of America
082022

ABOUT THE AUTHOR

William Arthur is a lifelong hockey fan who grew up playing the sport on a frozen pond in Thunder Bay, Ontario. He lives in northwest Ontario with his trusted foxhound.

TABLE OF CONTENTS

1

Mark Messier (rear right) celebrates after scoring in the 1994 Eastern Conference Finals.

CHAMPS AGAIN

New York Rangers fans needed something to believe in. If their team lost one more game in the 1994 Eastern Conference Final, the season would be over. Mark Messier wasn't worried. The team captain promised the Rangers would beat the New Jersey Devils in Game 6. Messier delivered. He scored a hat trick in a 4–2 win. The Rangers were still alive.

New York had won 52 games in the 1993–94 season. That was the most in the National Hockey League (NHL). The team cruised through the first two rounds of the playoffs. But what Rangers fans really wanted was the Stanley Cup. The team's last championship had been way back in 1940. New York hadn't even been to the Final since 1979. One more win against the Devils could end the drought.

The Rangers were 7.7 seconds away from victory in Game 7. That's when the Devils tied it 1–1. The New York crowd was stunned. However, the Rangers weren't about to crack. Messier was one of the NHL's most respected leaders. The veteran center calmed his

Stéphane Matteau (center) avoids a teammate's shot attempt in the 1994 Eastern Conference Final.

teammates. Early in the second overtime, Stéphane Matteau came through. The Rangers winger grabbed a loose puck. Then he skated around the Devils' net for a wraparound goal. New York was moving on.

Mark Messier lifts the Stanley Cup at the team's victory parade in New York City in 1994.

In the Final, the Rangers faced the Vancouver Canucks. New York jumped out to a 3–1 series lead. But the Canucks rallied back. The series went to Game 7. In the first period, star defenseman Brian Leetch scored first. A few minutes later, Adam Graves put the Rangers up 2–0. But it was Messier's second-period goal that sealed it. New York held on to win 3–2. As Messier lifted the Cup above his head, some fans in the arena cried with joy. They could celebrate their first Cup win in 54 years. The drought was finally over.

RUSSIAN FIRSTS

Russian players dominated international hockey for much of the 1900s. However, the Soviet Union didn't let them play in the NHL. That changed in 1989. Soon, Russians were dominating the league. Alexander Karpovtsev, Alex Kovalev, Sergei Nemchinov, and Sergei Zubov were members of the 1994 Rangers. They became the first Russians to have their names engraved on the Stanley Cup.

2

Tex Rickard
promoted boxing
matches for
heavyweight
champ Jack
Dempsey.

NEW YORK'S TEAM

In the early 1900s, Tex Rickard became wealthy by putting on boxing matches. Eventually, he became interested in hockey. In 1926, Rickard founded a new NHL team in New York City. He even had an arena for them to play in. Madison Square Garden had been the site of many famous boxing matches. Sportswriters nicknamed Rickard's new hockey team "Tex's Rangers." The nickname stuck.

A crowd gathers outside Madison Square Garden in 1929.

Another NHL team called the Americans already played in New York. But it didn't take long for the Rangers to become the city's favorite hockey team.

Rickard hired Conn Smythe as the team's general manager. Smythe left before the season started. But by that point, he had already put together a talented squad. Among the players were three future Hall of Famers. Meanwhile, Lester Patrick took over as general manager and coach.

The Rangers reached the Stanley Cup Final in 1928. Center Frank Boucher led the way. He scored four goals as New

LESTER PATRICK

Lester Patrick led New York to two Stanley Cups. In the 1928 Final, he even suited up for the Rangers as an emergency goalie. Patrick coached until 1939. He remained the team's general manager through 1946. Today, the Lester Patrick Trophy is awarded each year to a person who has made a major contribution to US hockey.

York defeated the Montreal Maroons. That made the Rangers the first American NHL team to win the Cup. New York won the Stanley Cup again in 1933 and 1940.

It was a glorious start for the Rangers. They were known for their tough but clean playing style. However, the league was less stable. Teams came and went. In 1942, the Americans folded. The NHL was left with only six teams. Those same six teams made up the league for the next 25 seasons.

Many hockey fans remember those years fondly. The league had many great players. Rivalries became intense. But it was not a successful period for New York. The Rangers came within one

The 1928 New York Rangers featured Lester Patrick (top row, third from left) and Frank Boucher (bottom row, third from left).

game of winning the 1950 Stanley Cup. Most years, though, they were one of the league's worst teams. However, big changes were on the way.

3

Rod Gilbert (left) celebrates with teammate Steve Vickers after scoring a goal.

BUILDING BACK

In the 1967–68 season, the NHL doubled in size to 12 teams. Meanwhile, a successful new era was beginning for New York. Starting in 1967, the Rangers reached the playoffs nine years in a row. They returned to the Stanley Cup Final in 1972. Hall of Fame winger Rod Gilbert had seven points in the Final. However, the Boston Bruins won the series in six games.

A new playoff streak began in 1978. It included another run to the Stanley Cup Final in 1979. This time, center Phil Esposito led the way. The Rangers won the first game of the Final. But the Montreal Canadiens took home the Cup.

In 1992, the Rangers reached the playoffs for the 14th time in 15 seasons. Once again, New York fell short of a championship.

Fans had reason to believe, though. Brian Leetch and Sergei Zubov were two of the league's great defensemen. If the puck got past them, goalie Mike Richter usually finished the job. Talented young wingers Adam Graves and Alex Kovalev were goal-scoring machines. Bringing

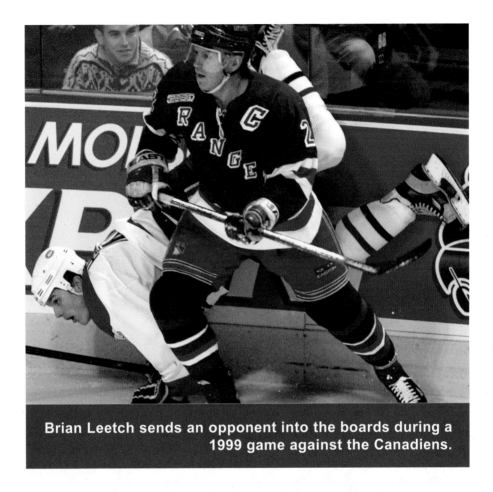

Brian Leetch sends an opponent into the boards during a 1999 game against the Canadiens.

them all together was veteran center Mark Messier.

The group had plenty of talent. They were also balanced and unselfish. And in 1993–94, they put together one of the

Sergei Zubov (left) hugs Glenn Anderson after Anderson scored in the 1994 Eastern Conference Final.

greatest seasons in Rangers history. It ended with the team's first Stanley Cup victory in 54 years.

Zubov left after that season. The rest of the core stayed together a little longer. The Rangers made another playoff run in 1997. This time they got to the conference final. Unfortunately for Rangers fans, it would be eight years before the team tasted playoff hockey again.

THE GREAT ONE ON BROADWAY

Wayne Gretzky earned his nickname "The Great One" in Edmonton. Playing beside Mark Messier, he led the Oilers to four Stanley Cups in the 1980s. Gretzky eventually ended his NHL career with the Rangers. The league's all-time leading scorer played three seasons in New York, from 1996 to 1999. True to form, he led the NHL in assists during two of them.

HENRIK LUNDQVIST

Goalie Henrik Lundqvist led his native Sweden to the 2006 Olympic gold medal. However, it was in New York where fans nicknamed him "King Henrik."

The Rangers picked Lundqvist 205th overall in the 2000 draft. Before long, he was an NHL star. As a rookie in 2005–06, he was among the league's top five in save percentage. Voters ranked him third for the Vezina Trophy. In 2012, Lundqvist won that award as the NHL's top goalie. In 15 NHL seasons with the Rangers, he set almost every team goalie record.

Standing 6-foot-1, Lundqvist was on the smaller side for goalies. However, he boasted lightning-quick reflexes. Playing deep in the crease, he had more time to react. Lundqvist was also known for his off-ice interests. These included fashion and playing guitar.

Henrik Lundqvist celebrates after a shutout in Game 6 of the 2014 Eastern Conference Final.

4

Jaromír Jágr tallied 319 points in his four seasons with the Rangers.

MARCHING
ON

By the early 2000s, the Rangers needed a reboot. It began in January 2004. That's when the team traded for Jaromír Jágr. The winger was one of the NHL's most dangerous scorers. Soon other skilled veterans joined the team alongside Jágr. Then, in October 2005, promising young goalie Henrik Lundqvist made his first start. The new-look Rangers

Ryan Callahan (right) roughs up an opponent during a 2012 game.

rode back into the playoffs after a seven-year drought.

The team's roster saw many changes in the coming years. Jágr left in 2008.

Fellow veterans Michael Nylander and Martin Straka had short stays too. Other skilled veterans came and went. However, a new core was forming.

The Rangers picked Ryan Callahan in the 2004 draft. The hardworking winger made his debut two years later. By 2011, he was team captain. Callahan played with high-scoring forwards Brad Richards and Rick Nash. Defenseman Ryan McDonagh added grit. Anchoring the group in net was Lundqvist.

The Rangers traded Callahan in 2014. In return, they got Martin St. Louis. The 38-year-old right winger was one of the league's best scorers. His leadership showed in the playoffs. New York met the

Chris Kreider acknowledges the New York crowd after a 4-0 win over the Columbus Blue Jackets in a 2021 game.

Pittsburgh Penguins in the second round. In Game 4, the Penguins jumped out to a 3–1 series lead. The next day, St. Louis's mother died. He left to be with his family. But he was back in action for Game 5. His teammates rallied behind him. They went on to complete the comeback in Game 7.

The Rangers kept the run going all the way to the Stanley Cup Final. The Los Angeles Kings eventually defeated the Rangers. But once again, New York was at the center of the hockey universe.

The Rangers struggled in the late 2010s and early 2020s. However, the team featured new stars such as wingers Chris Kreider and Artemi Panarin. Fans hoped it wouldn't be long before the Rangers were back on top.

MADISON SQUARE GARDEN

The Rangers play their home games at "The World's Most Famous Arena." The current Madison Square Garden opened in 1968. However, arenas bearing that name have stood in central Manhattan since 1874.

• NEW YORK RANGERS
QUICK STATS

FOUNDED: 1926

STANLEY CUP CHAMPIONSHIPS: 4 (1928, 1933, 1940, 1994)

KEY COACHES:

• Lester Patrick (1926–39): 281 wins, 216 losses, 107 ties

• Emile Francis (1965–73, 1974–75): 342 wins, 209 losses, 103 ties

• Alain Vigneault (2013–18): 226 wins, 147 losses, 37 overtime losses

HOME ARENA: Madison Square Garden (New York, NY)

MOST CAREER POINTS: Rod Gilbert (1,021)

MOST CAREER GOALS: Rod Gilbert (406)

MOST CAREER ASSISTS: Brian Leetch (741)

MOST CAREER SHUTOUTS: Henrik Lundqvist (64)

Stats are accurate through the 2020–21 season.

GLOSSARY

CREASE
The area directly in front of the goalie, painted in blue.

DEBUT
First appearance.

DRAFT
An event that allows teams to acquire new players coming into the league.

GENERAL MANAGER
The person in charge of a sports team, whose duties include signing and trading players.

HAT TRICK
A game in which a player scores three or more goals.

RIVALRIES
Ongoing competitions that bring out the greatest emotions between two players or teams.

ROOKIE
A professional athlete in his or her first year of competition.

VETERAN
A player who has spent several years in a league.

TO LEARN MORE

BOOKS

Duling, Kaitlyn. *Women in Hockey*. Lake Elmo, MN: Focus Readers, 2020.

Hewson, Anthony K. *Hockey Records*. Lake Elmo, MN: Focus Readers, 2020.

Omoth, Tyler. *A Superfan's Guide to Pro Hockey Teams*. North Mankato, MN: Capstone Press, 2018.

MORE INFORMATION

To learn more about the New York Rangers, go to **pressboxbooks.com/AllAccess**.

These links are routinely monitored and updated to provide the most current information available.

INDEX